Table Of Contents

Introduction

This book contains 250 messages for you, to read every morning before you start the day.

The messages are written and adapted to our complex lives and noisy world and the purpose Is to bring a little advice that can encourage you more towards self-love and towards the realization that you are a perfect and unique human being.

To enjoy this book, the messages should be read daily, not all at once.

We hope this book will bring you joy throughout the days and challenge you to focus more on yourself and to remember and keep in mind how amazing you truly are.

Keep up a positive attitude and don't let things in your past weight on you. Be proud that you rise every time, and this makes you a winner already.

Make today the day you take the first step towards your dream. Don't be scared by the magnitude of your goal and start with just one small action. Action is key. Remember that time goes by anyway and if you take one small step every day you will get there without even realizing it.

Remember that nothing is really free, and we pay for things with our time, with our life. Ask yourself if it is worth your time and sometimes it is ok to say no. No is a full sentence.

Spread love everywhere you go. Even the smallest gesture can make someone feel good. Don't miss on any opportunity to spread happiness.

Don't be a prisoner of your memories. Our memories are sweet, and we should treasure them, but we shouldn't let them keep us prisoners of the past. Be grateful for it and move on, keep on dreaming.

Life is beautiful when you focus on the positive. There is something good in everything if you carefully look for it.

Remember to smile today and every day! As time goes by, every smile will remain on your face and when you will be older you will look like you are smiling all the time.

We often forget to enjoy the little things and we get lost in every day's rush. Take a moment and remember to enjoy something small every day: a sunrise, a sunset, the chirp of a bird, the sun on your skin, the fresh smell of the morning.

Never stop traveling and take in the experiences and the beauty all around. Traveling can be a therapy for the soul, so why not do it more often?

Stop worrying. Visualize what you want and start feeling excited like it already happened. You have to feel it before you see it.

Never give up, keep on going and your perseverance will pay up sooner or later, usually when you least expect it. Consistency is key.

Today is the most important day of your life and the only important day. Make wise choices, stay in the present, enjoy your day and don't forget to have fun!

Today remember that you are capable, you are worthy, you are valuabe. Keep a wins journal and focus on the positive in everyday. What was your win today?

Don't be afraid to open your heart to people. Be proud of who you are and remember it's ok to be vulnerable from time to time.

Don't be too hard on yourself, celebrate every milestone and don't forget to relax. Praise yourself along the way.

Don't get so worried about security that you forget to live. Enjoy yourself while you are here. The Universe wants you to be happy and it has your back, so ask for guidance every morning.

Encourage others as you would encourage yourself and vice versa. You never know how much it can mean to them. See the good in everyone.

Love yourself first. Then you will be able to love others as well, even deeper than before.

Live your life from a place of love and you'll always be happy. Remember that hate is only hurting yourself, choose love every time.

Start your day by actually saying to yourself "I give myself permission to be happy today" and see for yourself how that works.

Travel is very powerful. Each place teaches us something new. Travel some place new as often as you can, it doesn't even have to be somewhere far.

Be a shining star no matter the situation. Remember that the stars keeps shining even when we can't see them. Never forget your worth!

No one is perfect nor should you try to be. Trying to be perfect will exhaust you and will make you unhappy. Also remember that perfect is boring.

Start planning today your next adventure, something that takes you out of your comfort zone. Do you love hiking, visiting a new city, skydiving, taking a cold bath in a nearby lake? Whatever it is, make sure you get out of your comfort zone at least once a year.

Take in the positive in everything. There is always something good in everything, even if it's just a lesson. Make it a habit to focus on the good.

Keep learning and you will stay young forever. Learning keeps your brain in shape, it makes you feel good about your new skill and you should definitely have fun while you do it.

Let your inner child be free! We never truly grow up, so say hi to him once in a while.

Start cleaning your spaces today. It doesn't have to be big, if it feels weird start with a list of what you could clean and go step by step. Clean your email, your contacts, your car, your mind, your heart. If you want new things in your life you have to make room for them.

No one can read your mind, don't assume people know what you need or what you want. Always communicate and it will save you lots of misunderstandings.

Become aware of your thoughts and always work on replacing negative thoughts with positive ones. It is not always easy, but you will succeed with practice. Remember that we become what we think, so choose your thoughts wisely.

Did you notice how each place has something beautiful? Today try to focus on the beauty that surrounds you and make a habit of it.

Try to make someone smile today. A nice gesture can turn on a chain of good which will touch many people. Be a spark in someone's day.

Be grateful to wake up every day. Now think of 5 things that make your life precious and be grateful for it. Do this every morning before you start your day for at least 21 days and notice the difference.

Reflect on the days that passed, see what you could have done better and also be proud of all that you have accomplished. Then go and enjoy yourself.

If someone doesn't have the same great vision as you, simply accept their opinion, but don't doubt yourself. Your imagination is powerful and it's the first place where you see your goals and dreams.

When you have good and positive thoughts not only that you look lovely, but your life will be lovely too.

When you have a bad experience, always ask yourself why did it come to you, what can you learn from it? Receive the answer and then let it go.

Start each morning visualizing your day. Then say no to everything else. Have a marvelous day!

You can't change yesterday, love it, accept it and let It be in the past. Today is a new day for you to live fully. Count your blessings and have a day full of gratitude.

Pay attention to see who your true friends are. Who is there to support you or comfort you when everyone else is busy? Who is honest with you and keeps you grounded, but is not hurting or disrespectful? You are lucky to have them.

Don't fall in love with someone's potential. Pay close attention to who they are now, don't love them for who you'd like them to be.

Weekends seem to disappear in a blink of an eye. Make the most of yours. It doesn't have to be something spectacular, it has to be something that you enjoy.

Don't let doubt and fear sneak in. Be patient and keep your faith. Keep your plans to yourself in the beginning and keep your faith high.

Better to fail than to ask yourself "what if". Go for it!

Live your life with good thoughts and good actions all the time. What you do everyday matters, and you never know when you have an impact.

Always remember to smile. The sun will come out again tomorrow. Don't try to calm the storm, calm yourself, the storm will pass. You can always control your attitude towards a situation.

Even if you spend the day alone, watch something that makes you laugh every day. Laughter is indeed a great medicine.

Filter the people in your life until the negative ones are at a minimum. Surround yourself with valuable people who support and accept you as you are.

If you wake up and you want to skip your morning routine or your meditation, remember that when you want to skip it, it's when you need it the most. You are better to the world when you take care of yourself first.

It isn't as bad as you sometimes think it is. It all works out. Don't put so much pressure on yourself. Get used to yourself being your biggest cheerleader.

Things to remember: you don't have to be perfect; having a bad day is ok; small steps are also progress; asking for help is strength; people love and appreciate you.

Even if sometimes is not easy, be selective with the people in your life. Don't live your life trying to justify yourself to people you do not need to justify yourself to. Your energy and you time are precious. Be with people who appreciate you for who you truly are and who put in the time and effort to know you.

Right now, think about what you are most grateful for at this moment in your life. Practice gratitude every day.

Hurting someone can be as easy as throwing a stone in the sea. But do you have any idea how deep that stone can go?

Learning from our own hurt and trauma, we should do our best and avoid hurting someone deliberately.

Take the time to put the camera away and marvel at what's in front of you. Life is better than on camera. You become the storyteller to pass on what you saw.

Believe in yourself and believe in better. What you believe in reflects in your actions and then it will reflect in your reality.

Take a moment to reflect on your latest choices and see if they take you closer to your dreams or maybe they reflect your fears. If they don't reflect your hopes and dreams, ask yourself what you could change starting now.

Never ever care what people would say. They are not walking in your shoes, and they don't live your life. Your first mission is to be true to yourself and live a life that makes you happy. This is the greatest gift you can give to the world.

For a healthy life, train both your mind and your body. To become a better person both personally and professionally you have to take care of your body, mind, soul and heart. Don't neglect any of it. All of it are you and you deserve the best. Allow yourself to have it.

Embrace change and allow people evolve and transform. Change is the only constant in this world. We need to grow, evolve, adapt and continuously become the best version of ourselves.

Don't judge other people because you don't know what they have been through. Chances are, if you would have lived their life, you would be in the exact same place they are. Be understanding and accepting.

What you focus your energy on, is what you will have more and more of in your life. Don't focus on the things and people you don't like. Focus on what you want to accomplish, focus on the good, focus on the positive, focus on the better and your life will become better.

When you become anxious, when you start panicking and even when you can't fall asleep, remember your breath and the power it has to bring you peace. Just breathe.

Stop overthinking everything and stop doubting yourself. Instead, think about all your great qualities, unique to you, that no one else has. Your superpower is being YOU. You are perfect.

When you have a bad day and you feel like you can't get out of bed, start your day with a meditation to clear your mind and then think about five things you are grateful for.

Do something today that will make you proud tomorrow. What is one action or one habit that you can start implementing today, that will take you closer to your goals?

When you lose your motivation think about your 'why'. When you know very well your 'why' you can always find your way back on the goal track.

To change your environment, you have to change yourself first. In life you receive what you are.

Unconditional love is the best gift you can give to yourself. Don't forget to be kind to yourself.

Tonight's forecast, 100% chance of fun and happiness. Let yourself be happy!

Your morning ritual will have the greatest impact on your day. So why not wake up early and start your day by meditating and being grateful?

Don't use your energy focusing on other people's lives. Don't allow yourself to be consumed by what other people are doing. Focus your energy on you, on your growth, on your blessings, on your dreams, on your life.

Make sure your happiness comes from within. You can't expect someone else to make you happy, like a fairytale savior. This is paving the path to disappointment. It's your responsibility to figure out how to be happy. Then, you can share happiness with someone else, but you can't expect someone to make you happy.

When you fall, remember you are strong enough to get up and move forward. Don't let anything and anyone convince you otherwise. You are amazing!

Move on from things and people who are not loving to you. Move on and live your best life. When in doubt, ask yourself, "is this loving to me?"

There is no such thing as ordinary people. We all have a piece of divinity in us. Each of us is unique and special. Embrace that!

Judge every day not by the results you see, but by the seeds you plant. Every seed counts.

Don't let your fears hold you back. Focus on the outcome and have faith the best will come.

Learn to be comfortable on your own, it is so empowering.

Say it out loud: I am strong, I am creative, I am smart, I believe in myself, I am enough.

Life is too short to tolerate things that don't make you happy. Start saying no once in a while, it's ok.

Learn to accept when you receive a gift, or when something good happens to you. Say thank you and be grateful. When you receive with an open heart and gratitude, the Universe will send you more.

When you don't approve of someone's behavior, remember that they are probably in pain, and at the end of the day we are all looking for the same thing in life: to be happy.

Stay kind and happy, you beautiful human.

Please set standards and boundaries for the people you want to keep in your life. It is a simple form of self-respect. And when you respect yourself, other people will follow.

Someday is code for never. Be stronger than your fear and start today. Turn one day in day one.

Behave the way you want the world to behave with you. Because whatever you plant in the Universe turns to you in some way.

Don't allow pain to stay with you longer than needed. Take your time and then use the pain to grow, turn it into wisdom.

A bad attitude can destroy us, but a positive one can save us and can also lead us to the life of our dreams. Choose your attitude wisely.

What famous and successful people have in common is that they didn't give up. They always got up and took another shot. Don't give up. When you feel like you can't take it anymore it means you are getting close. Keep moving forward.

No matter what you do there will always exist that one critic out there. You might as well follow your heart and do what makes you happy. When you stop caring about the critics, you become free.

Don't sit around waiting for an opportunity to come find you. Take action first and the opportunity will be revealed to you.

The ones who accept what they can't change, and they adapt, will survive no matter what.

Keep away from people who keep making fun of and laughing at your ambitions. Small people do that. Maybe it is not possible to keep them all away, then learn not to share your plans with everyone.

When you notice that you start criticizing yourself stop right there. Instead, compliment yourself and be understanding and forgiving of yourself.

Whenever you feel down, take some time to recover, you deserve a break. Don't feel guilty that you feel this way. It is normal. Even when you are a positive person and work on your personal growth, you will still get a day when you are overwhelmed. Allow your emotions to flow through you and take a little time for yourself.

Never forget how amazing you are. Be yourself because an original is always worth more than a copy. You are the hero in your life!

Learn to be more selfish. This means being less concerned of what people think of you, of what you do, how you live your life. Be selfish in a good way, be selfish in a healthy way for you.

You will never speak to anyone more than you speak to yourself in your head. Be kind to yourself. Consciously change the dialogue in your head and make it loving and positive.

The greatest happiness in life is to know that you are loved for who you are. Appreciate those who know you and love you.

We spend most of our time at work, so don't give up in finding the work you love. If you keep searching it will appear and it will all be worth it.

Take a moment now and be grateful to people who make you happy. Go as far as giving thanks to someone for being in your life.

To every action, there is an equal and opposite reaction. You may not see it right away, but keep this in mind and pay attention to your actions. The universal law takes care of everything.

Don't waste any breath. Live a meaningful life and always listen to your heart. You only have one chance at life, make it worth your while.

Travel is about the scenery, the people, the culture, the traditions. It's about so much beauty, your heart overflows with love. It is amazing to see how different one place is from another. How different traditions are. And among the differences, how similar we all are in our nature as human beings in our transitory journey on this planet.

Experiences enrich your soul like nothing else. What do you want to experience in the near future? Start planning now.

Fake it until you make it! We hear this so often. And don't forget to visualize the new reality you want to the smallest detail possible. See it and feel it as if it was already yours.

Start realizing how rare and valuable you are. You are unique and perfect just the way you ware.

Once you get to know and love people in more than
one place, city, country, the concept of home
becomes complex. But remember that at the end of
the day home is where the heart is.

When you do your own thing, you feel happy and
whole. Don't do it for attention or validation, do it
because it feels like the right thing for you to do.
When you live this way, you won't seek for validation
anymore.

Sometimes in love, compatibility is more important
than chemistry. Discuss your values, your goals,
your purpose and make sure you are looking
together in the same direction.

It's ok to feel disappointed and sad when things
don't work your way. Take your time, and then

remember to focus on the positive in every situation. There is a reason behind everything.

If you don't have anything nice to say to someone, better not say anything at all. Refrain from criticizing and hurting people.

Communication is the key to every misunderstanding. Always communicate and be honest about your intentions and your needs.

Be your best friend. Be your gym partner. Be your coffee buddy. Be your partner in crime. Be everything for yourself rather than relying on others to be that for you. Don't miss on your life only because at some moment there is no one free to be with you. Do your own thing, you are brave enough.

Learn to receive blessings with an open heart and be grateful for it. You deserve it.

If you love something, you should do it: dance, sing, paint, embrace your hobbies. Enjoy your life and enjoy yourself!

Stay away from the people who take you back to the habits you worked so hard to leave behind. Growing and improving yourself is normal and not everyone understands it.

Learn to dance in the storm. Get your umbrella and never stop dancing! You got this!

Another way to identify what we need to work on is to pay attention at what annoys us most in other people. Remember this and reflect on it next time it happens to you.

We are all different and there is no greater way of appreciation than accepting someone for who they are and appreciate those who accept us.

Before you leave the house say 5 things that you love about yourself and then go out into the world.

When you are content with yourself, the criticizing voices in your head will not matter anymore and will fade. Feel good in your skin.

Be thankful for closed doors, detours and roadblocks. They protect you from paths and places not meant for you. When something doesn't go as you hoped for, look at it as an opportunity to receive something better from the Universe and expect something great to happen.

In order to receive new things that you want, you need to get rid of the old things you don't need anymore. Clean your life and make room for new.

Be empathic even if you don't understand someone's pain. For them it is real. We all live, experience and feel differently.

Be grateful every day for what you have and this way you'll end up having more.

Take a decision today that will make you proud in 10 years. For example, drink more water, wear sun protection, or something else you think about.

Today, look at some pictures that bring back happy memories. Photography is the best tool to bring back moments otherwise gone, when our memory fails us. Celebrate your memories.

It's ok to be who you are, and it is never said enough. You are great just as you are.

Don't lose yourself waiting for closure to be given to you when you can give it to yourself. You are wonderful and capable of everything, and you can definitely get over something even without the closure you imagined.

Change is uncomfortable, but necessary. If you want to grow you have to be willing to change.

Don't be too hard on yourself. Try again tomorrow, sometimes this is what courage looks like.

People will never forget how you make them feel. If you don't believe it, think of some people that are or were part of your life and see how you remember them: by something they told you or how they made you feel?

Make a great appearance today and show everyone just how awesome you are.

Love yourself and don't compare yourself to others. Be the best YOU can be. The world loves authenticity.

When someone gets something wrong in a conversation don't jump at the occasion to correct them. If the correction is not important, you will only make them feel bad.

Love your life and life will love you back.

You need to ignore what everyone else is doing and achieving. Your only competition is you, stop comparing your life to someone else's. Compare yourself only with the person you were last year and see how much you have grown and achieved.

We are on this Earth to help each other. Be motivated by compassion, love, respect.

What is that one place you heard about so many times and you dream to see? Start to plan how you will make it happen. It is always better to see it for yourself than read about it endlessly.

Often the people closest to us get the worst of us. Try to be the best version of yourself for the people close to you. Remember how much you love them.

Unlearn destructive emotions, unlearn toxic behavior. Make a list of everything you need to unlearn and get to work.

Believe in miracles and they will happen. Each day be convinced that a miracle will happen for you, and you'll start to notice little synchronicities that will make you happy.

Some people focus on what they're getting, but the extraordinary ones think about who they're becoming. Do you like who you're becoming?

Take it chapter by chapter, stay in the present and let the future surprise you.

When you face a difficulty, take a break, take some distance and then look for the opportunity hidden inside of it and learn from it.

Not everyone will like you, and that is ok. Don't look for a reason and don't try to become a different person so that they will like you. Focus on becoming someone you like, because this is all that matters.

As you read and collect books, once in a while donate those you won't read a second time. Promote reading and help those who can't afford buying the books.

You can be a young 70-year-old or and old 20 year old. Don't let age define you. Keep your mind and soul young, embrace your inner child.

Be wise when choosing the people who get to be in your circle, not everyone deserves your time and energy. Protect yourself.

You never fail, you just get wiser through a process of elimination. Failure is sent to us to help us improve, become better and prepare us for success.

Stay curious and never be afraid to ask questions. Asking questions is an act of courage.

'I am brave.' Repeat it out loud in front of the mirror 3 times, like you mean it and believe it.

It's up to you to have a good day. Every morning decide to have a great day. Believe something good will happen for you today.

Be sure to have a good work - life balance. You need to work and serve the world, but don't forget to live your life and have fun at the same time.

If you are not satisfied with your life, revise your thoughts, your words, your actions, your habits and see where you need to start the change.

You are strong enough for everything life sends you. Take each day at a time and know you can do it.

Smile every day and laugh every day. Make it your daily mission and you will feel so good.

You are worthy, you are good enough, you are whole, you deserve all the good life has to offer.

Tough times never last and you are strong enough to get through. You've got this. Focus on the good and the good will get better.

Love yourself and the rest will follow. Remember you are your greatest treasure and your greatest responsibility, so put yourself first.

Don't ever save anything for a special occasion. Being alive is the special occasion. Eat the cake, drink the champagne, wear those fancy clothes, enjoy yourself any day.

When you start taking better care of yourself you start feeling better, looking better and you start to attract better. It all depends on you.

We live in a wonderful world that is full of beauty, opportunities, and adventure. What is the next adventure your soul desires?

When you seek to find out who you are, know that It's easier to identify who you are not, so start from there. It's all a process of elimination.

Remember you are worthy of all that you desire.

You only fail if you don't try again. Failure it's a choice. When you try again it makes you wiser.

You are a citizen of the world, and when you stop judging, you will begin to see God in everything and everyone. Start looking at the world with new eyes!

We must learn to press past our feelings. Acknowledge them and allow yourself to feel. Just don't get lost in it. Deal with it and move on.

Buy flowers to the ones you love and are still in your life. Don't wait for a special occasion to show your love and gratitude.

Realize that you are the hero you've been looking for. You are the main character of your life, and you should live accordingly.

You are powerful, you are genius, and you can achieve whatever you set your mind to.

If you don't like the direction your life is taking, change the rails. You have the power to design your life. You are the creator of your life.

When you are about to beat yourself up, stop for a moment and imagine you are talking to someone you love. What would you tell them? I am sure you would be loving, understanding, empathic. Only then, take your own advice.

Allow yourself to make mistakes. This is how we learn and grow. Never stop growing, because as you learn and grow you become conscious, and you learn to control yourself.

Your mind is incredibly powerful. Think positive thoughts every day and prepare yourself for a major change.

For your mind to work, you have to keep it open. Always upgrade your mindset and your thinking.

Old will not bring you something new. New behavior and new habits will bring you new results. This is your sign, stop waiting, today is the day. Do it.

Running doesn't make things disappear, you'll have to deal with it sooner or later. Better to face it now.

Be generous, humble and kind and you will attract similar people. You attract what you are.

You are a creator. Don't fall into the victim trap. Take a small step every day to improve your life. Remember that your thoughts are creating your reality. Choose them wisely.

Don't waste your energy trying to become someone society finds 'acceptable' or 'normal'. Focus on your growth and the person you want to be. Take care of your energy and don't be afraid to pause to recharge.

People don't fake depression, they fake being ok. Pay close attention to your friends and family and always be kind.

If you want to achieve peace you have to learn to let go. If it's not loving to you, don't hang on to it. Continue with your life. The best comeback is to be happy. Choose to be happy.

When a man starts travelling, the world is his house and all the people are his family. We are all a big family, so be kind to everyone.

Be brave today and every day. Expect a miracle today and every day! Be expectant of what you ask for and you shall receive.

Learn to be calm when you are disrespected. Your health will thank you. Be in control of your emotions.

If we could rewind time, we'd all be living in Groundhog day. Thank God you can get over it and live your life.

When you are at your lowest, life will teach you lessons that will help you get back to the top.

Take nothing personally. This is the healthiest thing to do. By now you know that someone's behavior has more to do with their suffering than it has to do with you.

Name five good things about today. Make it a habit to find the good in every day.

Action and faith will make your dream possible. Remember what your dream is and fight for it.

Trust yourself, your inner voice always knows better and if you keep listening to it, it will become more clear every time. Trust your intuition.

When people are hurting others, it's because they're hurting on the inside. Instead of being angry with these people, feel compassion for them instead and send them love.

Accept compliments without feeling uncomfortable, celebrate your strengths, release worry, smile more.

Life itself is a miracle. Look at everything in wonder. Look at the stars and the moon, how they shine for you in the sky.

Ask for what you want instead of assuming you can't have it. You might be surprised at the result.

When you stop learning you get left behind. Never stop educating yourself.

Nature has great energy and it is so impressive. Connect with nature, go out and feel the peace it gives you. Charge your energy in nature.

When you invest in travel, you invest in yourself. Never stop traveling.

Pick up a new habit that will bring you closer to excellence. What new habit can you start today?

In difficult times, don't react. Take your time to choose your response. You can only control yourself, not outside circumstances.

Don't get stuck in the past, life goes on anyway, and you'd better live yours.

Believe in yourself! You are smart, intelligent, strong, and unique. If other people can see this in you, you can definitely see it too.

More often than not, we learn from example more than we learn from words. Always try to be a good example and teach only through example.

Nothing can substitute experience. One day you'll understand why you had all the experiences you had and you'll end up loving them all.

We cannot become more than our own thought of ourselves. Work on this until you think the world of yourself.

You are amazing and it's time for you to see that. Make peace with who you are. The greatest freedom is to be yourself and loving it.

Know that fear will not disappear completely from your life. The secret is not to let it control you, act despite the fear. Say hello to it and leave it behind.

There are unlimited possibilities, unlimited solutions and unlimited ways around every single situation. Believe in it and look for it.

Start every day with the conviction that something great is going to happen to you and be expectant.

I can is an attitude. You can do whatever you put your mind to. Don't believe the negative voices in your head, they're just trying to protect you. Tell them that you, know they have good intentions, but you've got this and you can do it. You'll be ok.

Search for the beauty in everything, not for perfection. Perfect is a myth, but beauty and good are everywhere.

One of the greatest gifts you can give someone is thanking them for being part of your life. Make someone's day: call them and thank them for being part of your life.

Never put the key to your happiness in someone else's hands. You are enough to make yourself happy. Your happiness is your responsibility.

Listen to your heart, your intuition, and they will guide you until you find your path. Trust it!

If it doesn't make you happy, don't settle for it. You can create the life of your dreams.

Leave the past behind, live in the present and you'll end up having a surprising future.

Refrain from judging, our circumstances are different, and you never know how much someone else is hurting.

Be careful what you tolerate. You are teaching people how to treat you. It's ok to have boundaries and you should know yours and communicate it.

Learn how to walk away. When a connection starts to fade, learn how to let it go. When a person starts to mistreat you, learn how to move on to something and someone better. Don't waste your energy trying to force something that isn't meant to be. What's meant to be, it will be effortlessly.

When a negative thought enters your mind, think three positive ones. Train yourself every day to change to a positive mindset.

Distance yourself from people that bring out the person you're trying not to be anymore. Surround yourself with people that make you a better person.

Fall in love with someone who doesn't make you think love is hard. Love is the one thing in this world that does not hurt and it should be easy.

In life we don't get what we want, we get what we are. Be love, be abundant, be everything that you want to accomplish in your life.

In this life we have two families, the one that we are born into and one that we choose ourselves.

What you can't change shouldn't take up your time, your energy and your peace. If you can't do anything about it, then let it go.

Allow yourself to be proud of yourself and all the progress you've made, especially the progress no one else can see. Celebrate all your victories, even the small ones, you worked for it and you deserve it.

Fight your urges to complain and good things will happen when stop focusing on the problems. Talk about your joys more and more every day.

Take a moment to reflect on how much you have grown over this past year and celebrate all your hard work.

If you improve by 1% every day, within a year you'll have improved by 365%. Keep up the good work and you'll be unstoppable.

Work on being in love with the person in the mirror who has been through so much but is still standing and demonstrating success every single day.

It's important to realize that you are living inside one of your dreams while you wait for your next one. There's always a place for gratitude in our lives. And when we are grateful for the good things in our life we create more of the same.

Make a list of things that make you happy and make a list of things you do every day. If you want to improve your days, compare the lists and adjust accordingly until you fill your days with things that make you happy.

Imagination is the most powerful tool you have. Use your imagination to dream big and visualize only the best that you desire in your life. Don't let the worst-case scenarios run free in your mind. Instead of that, imagine the opposite and focus on the good that could happen. We are programmed to think the worst first, but you can change this using your imagination and seeing in your mind the opposite good scenarios in everything you want.

Choose to feel good and do good and this might just inspire others to do the same. When you do good you put in motion a chained reaction and unknowingly you touch so many lives.

Remember that you are your greatest investment, so treat yourself well: read books, expand your mind and enjoy every day. You have yourself for the rest of your life. Always, keep choosing you.

We attract what we are, not what we want. That's why we need to become great in order to build the great life we want and surround ourselves with great people.

Don't forget the best doctors in the world: food, sun, sleep, exercise, nature, laughter, hydration. Our bodies are a miracle, and we owe them to take care of them.

You can always control your thoughts and your attitude. Don't let outside events dictate how good of a day you will have. Decide now that today is going to be a great day.

A positive mindset is built with positive thoughts and positive talk. Focus on how you talk to yourself throughout the day and see how you can improve your inner dialogue.

Take care of your appearance, dress well, wear perfume, do your hair, even if you're just staying home. Be beautiful and elegant for yourself too, not only for the public.

Imagine where you would be in 6 months from now if you did one thing every day that got you closer to your goals. What is that one thing that you can start doing today?

You need people in your life that are more experienced, that are further along than you. You need to be exposed to new levels so you can grow and go to new levels.

It's the small habits: how you spend your mornings, how you talk to yourself, what you watch, what you read, who you spend your time with. This is what will change your life. Small habits are easy to implement in your life if you take the decision and commit to it.

Sometimes you need to risk it all for a dream only you can see. In the beginning keep your dreams to yourself and don't let outside voices influence you. You can do anything you want, you just have to build an image in your head first and then take action towards your vision.

You're inspiring people who you don't even realize are watching you. Just by showing up, being honest and sharing your value, you might give someone the courage to make a life changing decision. Keep being you at all times.

Don't rush anything. Everything comes to you in perfect timing. Keep having faith.

What if it does work out exactly how you imagined it or greater? Entertain that thought. Become obsessed with this thought.

Sometimes you have to remind yourself that you are special. That you can't be replaced: your heart, your mind, your company, your care. All of this can't be offered by someone else. You are unique and you are valuable to people.

Slow down, enjoy the process, trust the journey. Relax, master the day and then keep doing this every day.

Thank you.

Thank you for purchasing this book and for the trust you put in us.

Congratulations for finishing it!

We hope you enjoyed it and we truly hope it was helpful to you in some way or another.

Please let us know how you liked it at:

heianibooks@gmail.com

CPSIA information can be obtained
at www.ICGtesting.com
Printed in the USA
BVHW090407160222
629082BV00012B/1125